The Restaurant: From Concept to Operation

THIRD EDITION

udent Workbook

National Restaurant Association
EDUCATIONAL FOUNDATION

JOHN WILEY & SONS, INC.

New York • Chichester • Weinheim • Brisbane • Singapore • Toronto

ProMgmt. is a registered trademark of the National Restaurant Association Educational Foundation.

This student workbook is designed to be used with the textbook *The Restaurant: From Concept to Operation, Third Edition* by John R. Walker and Donald E. Lundberg.

This book is printed on acid-free paper.

Published by John Wiley & Sons, Inc.

Published simultaneously in Canada.

This publication is designed to provide accurate and authoritative information in regard to the subject matter covered. It is sold with the understanding that the publisher is not engaged in rendering professional services. If professional advice or other expert assistance is required, the services of a competent professional person should be sought.

Library of Congress Cataloging-in-Publication Data:

ISBN: 0-471-41310-0

Printed in the United States of America.

10 9 8 7 6 5

Contents

Introduction

The Restaurant: From Concept to Operation, Third Edition, will introduce a broad variety of restaurant functions. As future foodservice managers, you will find the overview useful both in planning future study and directing you toward satisfactory career choices.

The course begins with an overview of restaurant operations and then looks at menus, cost control, and financial matters. Legal issues, the restaurant staff, employee training, and equipping the kitchen are covered next. The course then discusses the fundamentals of marketing and purchasing and concludes with a section on customer service, laws and regulations, and sanitation.

How to Earn a ProMgmt℠ Certificate of Course Completion

To earn a ProMgmt. Certificate of Course Completion, a student must complete all student workbook exercises and receive a passing score on the final examination.

To apply for the ProMgmt. Certificate of Course Completion, complete the student registration form located on the inside back cover of this workbook and give it to your instructor, who will then forward it to the National Restaurant Association Educational Foundation.

Each student registered with the Educational Foundation will receive a student number. Please make a record of it; this number will identify you during your present and future coursework with the Educational Foundation.

ProMgmt. certificate requirements are administered exclusively through colleges and other educational institutions that offer ProMgmt. courses and examinations.

If you are not currently enrolled in a ProMgmt. course and would like to earn a ProMgmt. certificate, please contact your local educational institution to see if they are willing to administer the ProMgmt. certificate requirements for non-enrolled students. You can also visit **www.edfound.org** for a list of ProMgmt. Partner schools. ProMgmt. Partner schools offer seven or more courses that include administration of the ProMgmt. certificate requirements.

The Educational Foundation leaves it to the discretion of each educational institution offering ProMgmt. courses to decide whether or not that institution will administer the ProMgmt. certificate requirements to non-enrolled students. If an institution does administer ProMgmt. certificate requirements to non-enrolled students, that institution may charge an additional fee, of an amount determined by that institution, for the administration of the ProMgmt. certificate requirements.

Course Materials

This course consists of the text, *The Restaurant: From Concept to Operation, Third Edition*, by John R. Walker and Donald E. Lundberg, the student workbook, and a final examination. The examination is the final section of your course and is sent to an instructor for administration, then returned to the Educational Foundation for grading.

Each lesson consists of:
- Student objectives
- Reading assignment
- Chapter exercises

At the end of the workbook you will find:
- A study outline of the textbook
- A glossary (when the textbook does not have one)
- An 80-question practice test
- Answers to the practice test

The objectives indicate what you can expect to learn from the course, and are designed to help you organize your studying and concentrate on important topics and explanations. Refer to the objectives frequently to make sure you are meeting them.

The exercises help you check how well you've learned the concepts in each chapter. These will be graded by your instructor.

An 80-question practice test appears at the end of the workbook. All the questions are multiple-choice and have four possible answers. Circle the best answer to each question, as in this example:

Who was the first president of the United States?

    A. Thomas Jefferson.
    (B.) George Washington.
    C. Benjamin Franklin.
    D. John Adams.

Answers to the practice test follow in the workbook so that you may grade your own work.

The Final Exam

All examinations may first be graded by your instructor and then officially graded again by the Educational Foundation. If you do not receive a passing grade on the examination, you may request a retest. A retest fee will be charged for the second examination.

Study Tips

Since you have already demonstrated an interest in furthering your foodservice education by registering for this Educational Foundation course, you know your next step is study preparation. We have included some specific study pointers that you may find useful.

- Build studying into your routine. If you hold a full-time job, you need to take a realistic approach to studying. Set aside a specific time and place to study, and stick to your routine as closely as possible. Your study area should have room for your course materials and any other necessary study aids. If possible, your area should be away from family traffic.

- Discuss with family members your study goals and your need for a quiet place and private time to work. They may want to help you draw up a study schedule that will be satisfactory to everyone.

- Keep a study log. You can record what lesson was worked on, a list of topics studied, the time you put in, and the dates you sent your exercises to your instructor for grading.

- Work at your own pace, but move ahead steadily. The following tips should help you get the most value from your lessons.

1. Look over the objectives carefully. They list what you are expected to know for the examination.

2. Read the chapters carefully, and don't hesitate to mark your text—it will help you later. Mark passages that seem especially important and those that seem difficult, as you may want to reread these later.

3. Try to read an entire chapter at a time. Even though more than one chapter may be assigned in a lesson, you may find you can carefully read only one chapter in a sitting.

4. When you have finished reading the chapter, go back and check the highlights and any notes you have made. These will help you review for the examination.

Reviewing for the Final Exam

When you have completed the final exercise and practice test, you will have several items to use for your examination review. If you have highlighted important points in the textbook, you can review them. If you have made notes in the margins, check them to be sure you have answered any questions that arose when you read the material. Reread certain sections if necessary. Finally, you should go over your exercises.

The ProMgmt. Program

The National Restaurant Association Educational Foundation's ProMgmt. Program is designed to provide foodservice students and professionals with a solid foundation of practical knowledge and information. Each course focuses on a specific management area. For more information on the program, please contact the National Restaurant Association Educational Foundation at 800.765.2122 (312.715.1010 in Chicagoland) or visit our web site at **www.edfound.org**.

Lesson 1

STUDENT OBJECTIVES

After completing this lesson, you should be able to:

- Discuss reasons why some people open restaurants.

- List some liabilities of restaurant operation.

- Outline the history of restaurants.

- Compare the advantages and disadvantages of buying, building, and franchising restaurants.

- List and describe the various kinds and characteristics of restaurants.

- Compare and contrast chain and independent restaurant operations.

- Briefly describe the lives of prominent past and present restaurateurs.

- Discuss the contributions made by various chain, independent, and prominent restaurateurs.

Reading Assignment

Now read Chapters 1 and 2 in the text. Use this information to answer the questions and activities in Exercises 1 and 2.

Chapter 1 Exercise

1. List five reasons people have cited in choosing to open a restaurant, along with each reason's drawbacks.

   - _____
   - _____
   - _____
   - _____
   - _____

2. Foodservice employees often work long hours and are susceptible to
   A. poor financial decisions.
   B. weight gain.
   C. mononucleosis.
   D. repetitive motion injuries.

3. Some national restaurant chains expect managers to
   A. take weekends off.
   B. go on extended vacations.
   C. remain single.
   D. work fifty to seventy hours a week.

4. The original *restorantes* served by M. Boulanger in Paris were
   A. hot drinks made with rum.
   B. sugary desserts topped with chocolate sauce.
   C. special soups.
   D. casseroles made with sheep's feet.

5. The term "restaurant" gained popularity in Boston thanks to immigrants from
    A. England.
    B. Holland.
    C. France.
    D. Germany.

6. Often credited as the first American restaurant in the United States, Delmonico's was opened in which city?
    A. New York
    B. Atlanta
    C. San Francisco
    D. Chicago

7. Family-owned restaurants often succeed because
    A. they can be called Grandma's Place and she will actually be there.
    B. children in the family can legally be paid less than regular employees.
    C. there is a ready-made clientele for the restaurant.
    D. the general public likes watching families working together and will come more often.

8. When buying an existing restaurant, it is best to choose one that is at least
    A. one year old.
    B. three years old.
    C. five years old.
    D. ten years old.

9. The International Franchise Association's list of restaurant concepts has more than
    A. 500 registered concepts.
    B. 1,000 registered concepts.
    C. 2,500 registered concepts.
    D. 5,000 registered concepts.

10. Buying a franchise

    A.   eliminates the risk of failing.

    B.   reduces the risk of failing.

    C.   ensures the restaurant will do well in your location.

    D.   comes with free advertising.

11. The National Restaurant Association projects that jobs in foodservice will

    A.   increase over the next five years.

    B.   decrease over the next five years.

    C.   remain the same over the next five years.

    D.   require a graduate degree from a culinary institute by the year 2006.

Chapter 2 Exercise

1. The most popular eateries in the United States are
    A. family dining operations.
    B. hamburger chains.
    C. fried chicken chains.
    D. Italian restaurants.

2. Food costs are typically lower in Mexican restaurants because
    A. only a small percentage of meat is used.
    B. spicy foods increase beverage sales.
    C. fewer people eat there.
    D. flour tortillas can be used as plates to hold food.

3. Fine dining restaurants invest heavily in
    A. humorous television commercials.
    B. computer systems to speed up food delivery and table turnover.
    C. public relations campaigns.
    D. drive-thru windows and other take-out services.

4. The cost of seafood is expected to decline in the future due to
    A. overfishing.
    B. a reduction in consumer demand.
    C. mom and pop operations being bought by national chains.
    D. advances in aquaculture.

5. The largest number of ethnic restaurants in the United States are
    A. Italian.
    B. Thai.
    C. Irish.
    D. French.

6. If the menu offers green spinach pasta noodles, the restaurant is probably

   A. Indian.

   B. French.

   C. Chinese.

   D. Northern Italian.

7. Szechwan cooking is best known for its use of

   A. hot peppers.

   B. marinated steaks.

   C. cream-based soups.

   D. bite-sized dumplings.

8. Restaurants that spend more on decoration than food quality are usually referred to as

   A. ethnic restaurants.

   B. theme restaurants.

   C. burger joints.

   D. luxury establishments.

9. A large portion of profits at theme restaurants are derived from

   A. merchandise sales.

   B. local residents.

   C. leasing the venue as a movie location.

   D. fine wine sales.

10. Chef-owned operations often fail because

   A. they believe their name alone will draw customers.

   B. they don't have the business skills to run the restaurant.

   C. a marital dispute leads to divorce and a split of the assets.

   D. all of the above.

11. The best thing chef-owners can do to ensure success is
    A.   learn everything possible about their favorite cuisine.
    B.   develop recipes that are distinctive.
    C.   find someone to assist with business management.
    D.   get publicity photos taken.

12. An in-between bakery/café approach features
    A.   homemade products of highly skilled, on-site bakers who begin work around 3 a.m.
    B.   products fully produced elsewhere and delivered to the site.
    C.   products prepared elsewhere, delivered to the site, and baked at the site.
    D.   products prepared centrally and delivered to the site, then final proofed and baked at the site.

13. Howard Johnson's restaurants built their reputations by
    A.   serving twenty-eight flavors of high-quality ice cream.
    B.   offering home-delivery services.
    C.   incorporating aquariums into their décor.
    D.   selling homemade pecan rolls.

14. Alice Waters' restaurant Chez Panisse became profitable in its
    A.   first year.
    B.   third year.
    C.   eighth year.
    D.   tenth year.

15. List three characteristics shared by the restaurateurs profiled in Chapter 2.
    - _____
    - _____
    - _____

Lesson 2

Student Objectives

After completing this lesson, you should be able to:

- Realize the advantage of a good restaurant name.

- Explain the relationship between concept and market.

- Be able to write a restaurant concept.

- Understand restaurant knockout criteria.

- Develop a marketing and business plan.

- Conduct a market assessment.

- Discuss the importance of the four Ps of the marketing mix.

- Describe the best promotional ideas for your restaurant.

Reading Assignment

Now read Chapters 3 and 4 in the text. Use this information to answer the questions and activities in Exercises 3 and 4.

Chapter 3 Exercise

1. List five factors that help project a restaurant's concept to the target market.

   - _____
   - _____
   - _____
   - _____
   - _____

2. The Hard Rock Café, Victoria Station, and Papagus are all examples of what kind of restaurants?

   A. Quick service

   B. Theme

   C. Dinner house

   D. Chef-owned

3. Why might a successful restaurant become unprofitable after a number of years?

   _____

4. What is the advantage of opening a multiple-concept chain?

   _____

   _____

5. Instead of national advertising campaigns, most fine dining establishments spend more on what to promote their restaurants?

   _____

6. Why might a takeover location be desirable for a new restaurant owner?

   _____

   _____

Chapter 4 Exercise

1. Why is a marketing plan critical to the success of a restaurant? Who will see it and why?

   _____

   _____

2. Match the following terms with their meaning:

   _____(1) Marketing plan

   _____(2) Marketing strategy

   _____(3) Market assessment

   _____(4) Market potential

   a.   Defines the number of customers, near or far, that might visit the restaurant.

   b.   Identifies the target market and its needs and explains how to meet these needs.

   c.   Analyzes the community, customers, and competition

   d.   Positions the restaurant in relation to the competition.

3. Are the following advertising (A), public relations (PR), or promotions (P) activities?

   _____(1) Purchasing a quarter-page space in a newspaper

   _____(2) Appearing on a national talk show to demonstrate cooking techniques

   _____(3) Donating dinner for four to a charity auction

   _____(4) Handing out food samples at a community festival

   _____(5) Paying for the uniforms of a youth soccer team

   _____(6) Judging the pie-baking contest at the county fair

   _____(7) Mailing two-for-one coupons to senior citizens

   _____(8) Putting two-for-one coupons in the local newspaper

   _____(9) Organizing a food drive for a nearby homeless shelter

   _____(10) Announcing a new menu item on the radio

4. Communicating to the target market the benefits of a restaurant is _____, whereas servers promoting the daily special are _____.

Lesson 3

Student Objectives

After completing this lesson, you should be able to:

- Know what it takes to acquire a loan in order to start a restaurant.

- Discuss the strengths and weaknesses of various types of loans available to restaurant operators.

- Explain the nuances of restaurant leases.

- Evaluate various forms of business ownership and decide which is best for your restaurant.

- Discuss the advantages and disadvantages of each form of business.

- Realize the legal aspects of doing business.

- Plan a restaurant menu.

- Price a restaurant menu.

- Decide how to lay out and design a restaurant menu.

Reading Assignment

Now read Chapters 5–7 in the text. Use this information to answer the questions and activities in Exercises 5–7.

Chapter 5 Exercise

1. A large number of restaurants fail because they do not have a sufficient amount of what to remain in business for more than their first year?

   _____

2. To conserve capital, owners often make which two arrangements for the building and land?

   _____

3. Name the term for assets bankers, to reduce their risk when lending money, require borrowers to pledge in case the borrower can't repay the loan.

   _____

4. Because restaurants take a long time to construct, it is best to negotiate what before the first rent payment is due?

   _____

5. Name the three principal parties involved in an SBA-guaranteed loan.

   - _____

   - _____

   - _____

6. Most loans rejected by the SBA are due to what kind of financial information?

   _____

7. Banks will accept what on land or what on equipment as collateral?

   _____

8. After completing an SBA loan application, it should be delivered where for approval?

_____

9. How can a future business owner be prepared with the right documentation needed to submit a loan application?

_____

10. What document shows a lender that a borrower has the ability to run a successful restaurant?

_____

11. Name three things lenders look at closely to determine an applicant's character.

- _____

- _____

- _____

12. What kind of building and equipment arrangement can be troublesome if the restaurant closes before the expiration of this contract?

_____

13. What are the three owner expenses meant by the term CAMs?

- _____

- _____

- _____

14. One clause in a lease should state that the lease is void if what cannot be obtained?

_____

15. What are a restaurant's two potential values?

* _____

* _____

Chapter 6 Exercise

1. List three basic types of business organizations.

   - _____

   - _____

   - _____

2. What are some of the advantages and disadvantages of operating a restaurant as a sole proprietor?

   _____

   _____

3. Why are restaurants operating as corporations double taxed and what can owners do to avoid this situation?

   _____

   _____

4. Why is it better from a tax perspective to put money into a corporation as a loan rather than as stock?

   _____

   _____

5. How can two corporations own one restaurant, and what is the tax advantage for this strategy?

   _____

   _____

   _____

True or false.

_____6. The cost for attending a restaurant trade show is fully tax deductible.

_____7. By law, children in a family-owned restaurant do not need to be paid until they are age 18.

_____8. Anyone who works more than forty hours in a single week must be paid overtime for the extra hours.

_____9. The Federal Equal Pay Act prohibits employers from discriminating on the basis of age or race.

_____10. The most effective way to prevent sexual harassment is the adoption and dissemination of a sexual harassment policy.

_____11. It is the seller's responsibility to sell alcoholic beverages only to those people legally entitled to buy.

_____12. If a server serves alcohol to a minor, it is the restaurant owner who is solely responsible for any problems that occur.

_____13. As long as they do not serve food, musicians are always considered contract employees by the law.

_____14. Only businesses that choose to be corporations need to have a taxpayer identification number.

Chapter 7 Exercise

1. What are some of the major challenges a restaurant owner faces when planning a new menu?

   _____

   _____

2. Why is the menu considered so important to the success of a restaurant?

   _____

   _____

3. How can a restaurant ensure all menu items have the right weight, shape, and taste, as described in the menu?

   _____

   _____

4. In what ways are restaurants trying to meet increasing customer demand for more nutritious menu items?

   _____

   _____

5. When restaurants are short on kitchen space, what items are often purchased off site?

   _____

6. Patrons often consider what more important than service, value, or cleanliness?

   _____

7. Fluctuations in food prices can be overcome by developing what kind of menus?

   _____

8. What two things determine the parameters of menu prices?

• _____

• _____

9. The difference between what a food item costs and what is charged is called the

_____.

10. Name the menu type that is a sample of the chef's best dishes.

_____

11. What type of menus allow guests to create a complete meal at a fixed price?

_____

_____

12. When La Cuisine d'Or switched to a new menu, sales of its most popular item fell dramatically. Why might this have happened, and what could management have done to avoid this problem?

_____

_____

_____

_____

_____

Lesson 4

Student Objectives

After completing this lesson, you should be able to:

- Explain how to obtain an alcoholic beverage license.

- Assist in the planning of a bar setup.

- Suggest wines to accompany menu items.

- Know the restaurant's liability under the law regarding the sale of alcoholic beverages.

- List ways in which bartenders and others can defraud the restaurant bar and beverage operation.

- Establish standards for purchasing restaurant food items.

- Determine how to set up a basic restaurant purchasing system.

- Establish par stocks and reordering points.

- Operate a basic restaurant purchasing system.

Reading Assignment

Now read Chapters 8 and 9 in the text. Use this information to answer the questions and activities in Exercises 8 and 9.

Chapter 8 Exercise

1. What role do state departments of alcohol beverage control play in the restaurant industry?

   _____

   _____

2. What two main types of liquor licenses do restaurants use?

   • _____

   • _____

3. Why are beverage (bar) sales important to a restaurant?

   _____

   _____

4. What factors are involved in choosing the bar's location inside the restaurant?

   _____

   _____

5. What techniques are used by designers to make a bar more inviting?

   _____

   _____

6. When a customer asks for a red wine, even though he or she is ordering fish, what should the server do?

   _____

   _____

7. Aside from mixing drinks, list three major responsibilities of a bartender.

- _____

- _____

- _____

8. In what way can dram shop legislation or third-party liability be devastating for a restaurant?

_____

_____

9. Even if a restaurant has never experienced a problem with its alcohol sales, why should managers establish a responsible alcohol service program?

_____

_____

10. What are some of the best ways to control losses from the bar area?

_____

_____

_____

Chapter 9 Exercise

1. What are the five factors that must be determined to develop a food purchasing system?

   - _____
   - _____
   - _____
   - _____
   - _____

2. How does the manager ensure the right quality of food is delivered to the restaurant?

   _____

   _____

3. What is the difference between par stock and the re-order point?

   _____

   _____

4. Why do purchasers hold annual can-cutting tests?

   _____

   _____

5. Managers often request daily price quotes for what types of food?

   _____

   _____

6. What stock-rotation system do most restaurants use to minimize spoilage in their storerooms?

_____

7. What issues must a manager look at when purchasing meat?

_____

_____

8. How can managers cut the cost of eggs without reducing the restaurant's food quality?

_____

_____

9. Why can fresh fruits and vegetables be expensive, and what are some methods purchasers use to limit their reliance on fresh produce?

_____

_____

10. How can a restaurant owner reduce the cost of coffee?

_____

_____

Lesson 5

PLANNING AND EQUIPPING THE KITCHEN AND BUDGETING AND CONTROLLING COSTS

Student Objectives

After completing this lesson, you should be able to:

- Plan a basic kitchen layout.

- Determine what kitchen equipment is appropriate for your restaurant.

- Prepare for a health department inspection.

- Forecast sales.

- Prepare an income statement.

- Prepare a financial budget for your income.

- Establish a cash flow budget.

- Identify requirements as a basis to determining the appropriate computer system for a restaurant.

Reading Assignment

Now read Chapters 10 and 11 in the text. Use this information to answer the questions and activities in Exercises 10 and 11.

Chapter 10 Exercise

1. What is the basic goal of kitchen planning?

   _____

   _____

2. What is the shape of the most efficient kitchen layout?

   _____

3. What is the number one cause of restaurant accidents?

   _____

4. Which griddle allows cooks to prepare a wide range of foods on one piece of equipment?

   _____

5. Name four cooking techniques possible using a tilting skillet.

   - _____
   - _____
   - _____
   - _____

6. When filled with water, what piece of cooking equipment can be used to blanch vegetables?

   _____

7. What type of oven relies on radiated energy rather than heat to cook foods?

   _____

8. What piece of cooking equipment allows cooks to replace hot air with cold water to quickly stop the cooking process?

_____

9. Why is equipment maintenance so important?

_____

_____

10. What problems can occur when the dishwasher breaks down?

_____

_____

_____

_____

11. Match each piece of equipment with the kitchen area where it is normally found. Note that some letters will be used more than once.

_____(1) Disposer	a. Storage
_____(2) Can opener	b. Pre-preparation
_____(3) Coffee maker	c. Cooking
_____(4) Refrigerator	d. Serving
_____(5) Steamer	e. Cleanup and Sanitation
_____(6) Range	
_____(7) Dishwasher	
_____(8) Griddle	
_____(9) Salamander	
_____(10) Infrared lamp	

Chapter 11 Exercise

1. Match the numbered terms with the lettered definitions.

    _____(1) Sales

    _____(2) Sales forecasting

    _____(3) Cost of sales

    _____(4) Net income

    _____(5) Gross profit

    _____(6) Fixed costs

    _____(7) Variable costs

    _____(8) Average guest check

    _____(9) Guest count

    _____(10) Cash flow

    _____(11) Current ratio

    a. All money paid out to finance the restaurant

    b. All money remaining after all bills are paid

    c. All assets divided by outstanding debts

    d. Expenses that change depending on sales volume

    e. Total sales divided by the number of patrons

    f. All money available to pay bills

    g. Total amount of money received from all guests

    h. All money received before any bills are paid

    i. An educated prediction of the success or failure of the restaurant

    j. Expenses that remain constant over long periods of time

    k. Total number of patrons over a specific period of time

2. A well-designed computer system can do most calculations managers need to efficiently run a restaurant. In what other ways can data collected by a computer help improve a restaurant's profitability?

    _____

    _____

Lesson 6

THE HUMAN SIDE OF BUSINESS AND FOOD PROTECTION AND SANITATION

Student Objectives

After completing this lesson, you should be able to:

- Draw up task and job analyses for each position in a restaurant.

- Develop job descriptions for each position in a restaurant.

- Know which interview questions are appropriate, and which are not.

- Plan and conduct an orientation.

- Develop a training program.

- Establish restaurant foodservice policies and procedures.

- Know how to take guest food and beverage orders.

- Set up procedures for dealing with various situations.

- Develop and maintain a food protection system.

- Discuss the various types of food poisoning and how to prevent them.

Reading Assignment

Now read Chapters 12–15 in the text. Use this information to answer the questions and activities in Exercises 12–15.

Chapter 12 Exercise

1. List five tasks that should be included in a job description for a server.

    • _____

    • _____

    • _____

    • _____

    • _____

2. What is the difference between a job description and a job specification?

    _____

    _____

3. What is a job instruction sheet, and who uses it?

    _____

    _____

4. How has the Americans with Disabilities Act (ADA) affected the restaurant industry?

    _____

    _____

5. List three areas in a restaurant where minors under the age of 16 cannot work.

    • _____

    • _____

    • _____

6. What hiring objectives should a manager consider when hiring a new employee?

    _____

    _____

7. Indicate whether each of the following interview questions is legal (L) or illegal (I). Note that each letter will be used more than once.

_____(1) Are you married?

_____(2) Are you old enough to work here?

_____(3) Where were you born?

_____(4) What year did you graduate from high school?

_____(5) How long were you at your last job?

_____(6) How many hours a week are you looking for?

_____(7) What church do you go to?

_____(8) Who should I contact in case of an accident?

_____(9) What was the most enjoyable part of your last job?

_____(10) Were you let go from your last job?

Chapter 13 Exercise

1. Why is a having well-planned orientation program important?

   _____

   _____

2. Why is the time-tested process of learning by following not always successful when training new employees?

   _____

   _____

3. What is the importance of emphasizing employee development?

   _____

   _____

4. Why should training be spaced out over a period of a few days or weeks, rather than completed in a few quick sessions?

   _____

   _____

5. What are the benefits of learner-controlled instruction (LCI)?

   _____

   _____

6. How should a manager react to a difficult situation?

   _____

   _____

7. How should a manager react to these examples?

   a.   A server, rushing through the kitchen, collides with a prep cook, knocking a large bowl of prepared food to the floor.

   _____

   _____

   _____

   b.   An exceptionally boisterous crowd has just left the restaurant and the server has worked very hard to keep them happy.

   _____

   _____

   _____

   c.   The wrong person accepted delivery of a crate of produce.

   _____

   _____

   _____

Chapter 14 Exercise

1. What is the number one reason people do not return to a restaurant?

_____

2. As what, with two shows a day, do most servers see themselves?

_____

3. What kind of service is usually wanted by customers traveling alone?

_____

4. List the two types of work mindsets detrimental to the service quality of a restaurant, and explain their problems.

- _____

   _____

- _____

   _____

5. Who is the person to promote menu items directly to the customer?

_____

6. The server's job is to do what to the customers' entire dining experience?

_____

7. When a customer complains, when should the manager respond?

_____

8. What restaurant staff member sets the tone for the entire dining experience?

_____

9. When dealing with a difficult customer, explain why it is important to:
- be diplomatic

- remain calm

- listen carefully

- empathize

- control your voice

- obtain all the facts

- respond immediately

Chapter 15 Exercise

1. What are the three types of hazards to safe food?

    • _____

    • _____

    • _____

2. The biological hazard that causes infection comes from _____.

3. The biological hazard that uses food as a means of transportation is called
   a _____ .

4. Which foods are responsible for most foodborne illnesses?

   _____

   _____

5. What can each employee do to reduce the chance of an outbreak of foodborne
   illness in his or her restaurant?

   _____

   _____

6. Why is temperature so important in the control of bacteria?

   _____

   _____

7. Why are microwave ovens not used more often in restaurants?

   _____

   _____

8. Why should detergents be carefully marked and stored near the dishwashing area?

_____

_____

9. What does HACCP stand for, and why is the system so important?

_____

_____

10. Give two examples of cross-contamination: one in the kitchen and one in the dining room.

   • _____

   • _____

11. How long does it take to thoroughly clean hands?

_____

12. Why should someone who appears to be healthy still be concerned with his or her personal hygiene?

_____

_____

13. What are some reasons for hiring a licensed pest control operator?

_____

_____

14. What is the long-range goal of the Integrated Pest Management (IPM) program?

_____

_____

Study Outline

Chapter 1

1. People open restaurants because it is interesting and challenging, and offers the potential to make investors wealthy.

2. Successful restaurateurs need considerable experience, planning, financial support, and energy.

3. Restaurant owners cite steady hard work and the ability to work well with people as the two major keys to their success.

4. Excessive fatigue from long hours working in a restaurant can jeopardize a person's emotional and physical well-being.

5. There is often little job security for managers working for others, since a change in ownership often means management will be replaced.

6. The term "restaurant" is derived from the restoratives served by M. Boulanger in 18th-century Paris.

7. In 1794 Jean-Baptiste Gilbert Paypaolt opened the first foodservice establishment called a restaurant in Boston. However, because of its style, New York City's Delmonico's, which opened in 1827, is often credited as the first American restaurant.

8. The financial risk of opening a restaurant is staggering, since new foodservice businesses fail at a higher rate than new businesses in other industries. Many of these startups have successful concepts but lack the funds to stay open long enough to establish the business.

9. Family-owned restaurants often succeed because family members can work for lower salaries, and they reduce the risk of theft. However, stress from long hours at work and differences of opinion often cause families to splinter.

10. Statistics show that restaurants that remain open for at least three years have the best chance for survival.

11. Before deciding whether to buy, build, franchise, or manage someone else's restaurant, it is necessary to consider a host of factors, including economic conditions, potential market, competition, and capital available from investors.

12. Buying an existing restaurant reduces risk, since many weaknesses of the existing business can often be overcome.

13. Building a new restaurant requires the largest financial investment. At the same time, it offers the greatest potential for self-expression and personal fulfillment.

14. Franchising has the **least risk,** since the concept has already been tested, but it offers owners very little flexibility.

15. Managing a restaurant for an owner involves the **least financial risk,** but can still be emotionally draining if the restaurant fails.

Chapter 2

1. Restaurants are broadly classified as quick-serve, family, casual, dinner house, and fine dining.

2. The types of restaurants are constantly changing and today's market leaders may not even exist in the future.

3. The most successful leaders in the restaurant industry usually are hardworking and willing to learn from their mistakes, and take full advantage of their natural public relations skills.

4. Quick-serve restaurants aim to serve the maximum number of patrons in the least amount of time.

5. Quick-serve restaurants depend on national and local advertising to reach their target markets.

6. Mexican-style food is relatively inexpensive because of the small percentage of meat used, reducing food costs.

7. Despite higher-than-average food costs, steakhouse owners often choose to open this type of restaurant because it offers a limited menu and caters to an easily-defined market.

8. Customers in fine dining establishments expect all food, drink, and service to be of the highest quality and are willing to pay extra for it. The entire dining experience must stimulate the visitor's visual, auditory, and psychological senses.

9. Historically, ethnic restaurants were small and family owned, but over the past ten years some have grown to become national chains.

10. Theme restaurants are built around an idea with a focus on fun and fantasy. They have a short life cycle and often earn a large portion of their profits from merchandise sales.

11. Chef-owned operations benefit from having a highly experienced and very motivated person in charge but often suffer because the chefs don't have the business knowledge to manage the financial side.

12. A number of women have succeeded in the restaurant business. According to the National Restaurant Association, women held 68 percent of all supervisory positions in 1999.

13. Bakery/cafés serve coffee as well as fresh baked goods. Today, many of them manufacture their baked goods at central commissaries, then finish the baking process on site.

14. Due to the Internet, the volume of home delivery is expected to increase as well as grow from primarily pizzas to include full dinners.

15. Travel centers are often located miles from the nearest town and offer a wide range of food services for travelers.

Chapter 3

1. Successful foodservice establishments begin with a clear restaurant concept that projects the new restaurant's image. The concept must entice the desired audience and do it in a way that is different and better than the competition.

2. When choosing a concept, be sure there is a market to support it and a market gap, or need, for the concept offered.

3. The restaurant's name, décor, atmosphere, menu, logo, style of service, and everything else associated with the operation stems from, and should reflect, the original concept.

4. No restaurant concept is completely new, only modified or improved upon from existing operations.

5. Restaurants have a natural life cycle: birth, growth, maturity, senescence, and death. They often fall into decline due to a change in demographics or when the concept falls out of favor with the public.

6. If a restaurant is failing, adapting the concept to fit the market can often save it.

7. A single-concept chain stays with just one successful concept, theme, and niche. A multiple-concept chain profits from several different concepts.

8. Different types of foodservice operations require different levels of service based on many factors, including expected seat turnover rate.

9. Once the concept has been developed, more concrete decisions must be made concerning expected seat turnover rates, space needed per customer, menu prices, marketing strategies, and other aspects of the business.

10. Restaurant owners often write mission statements to solidify for themselves and their employees the company's business goal. A mission statement should include:

    a. the purpose of the enterprise;

    b. its business strategy;

    c. behavior standards it will follow; and

    d. values the management and employees will adhere to.

11. The right location for a restaurant is determined in large part by the restaurant's concept. A quick-service restaurant must be easily accessible, whereas diners looking for a special occasion are more willing to search out the location.

12. The following factors must be evaluated when choosing a site for a restaurant:

    a. demographics of the area: age, occupation, religion, family size, and average income in the community;

    b. visibility and accessibility for foot and car traffic;

    c. number of potential customers traveling through the area;

    d. distance from the potential market; and

    e. desirability of surroundings.

13. Owners must investigate existing and future zoning rules for the site before making a final decision.

14. When any reason is found not to open on a particular site, it is called a knockout criterion. The location should be abandoned and another one investigated.

15. An excellent way to learn the layout of an area is to use a topographical survey.

16. The décor of a restaurant is critical to its success. The most important aspects are the lighting design and the colors chosen to reflect the restaurant's concept.

Chapter 4

1. Marketing plans help owners identify their target market, assess their needs and desires, and develop strategies to meet these needs. Information about the targeted group is called a market assessment.

2. It is necessary to determine benefits the restaurant provides that are not offered by competitors and communicate this advantage to attract potential customers.

3. To determine and promote a restaurant's competitive advantage, managers should develop a marketing strategy based on the four Ps.

   a. Price—should be within the range expected by the target market, but still high enough to remain profitable.

   b. Product—excellent food, service, and atmosphere that meet the demands of the target market.

   c. Place—must be visible, accessible, and convenient.

   d. Promotion—communicating benefits the restaurant offers to the target market through advertising.

4. Regardless of the type of advertising a restaurant chooses to use, it must be appropriate for the target market and induce customers to visit the restaurant often.

Chapter 5

1. Even though poor management is cited as the reason for a restaurant failure, for many owners, insufficient financing and a shortage of working capital also play major roles in the operation's demise.

2. It is not necessary to own the entire restaurant. Experienced owners often rent or lease the land and building, then secure financing to purchase equipment and have access to working capital.

3. Operators can borrow capital from a bank, savings and loan, private lenders, limited partners, or the Small Business Association (SBA).

4. Securing an SBA loan is a four-step process which requires:

   a. obtaining a list of participating banks;

   b. submitting a completed applications to a member bank;

   c. waiting for the local SBA to approve the loan; and

   d. visiting the lender to sign the loan documents.

5. Lenders want to see a carefully thought out business plan showing that funds will be put to work as soon as capital becomes available.

6. The borrower must have collateral, or hard assets, to secure a loan. Lenders will also evaluate a prospective borrower's character to determine his or her creditworthiness.

7. New restaurant owners may choose to lease the building and equipment because it requires less capital. However, if the business fails before the lease expires, the owner is still responsible for all outstanding lease payments.

8. When drawing up a lease agreement, a number of critical issues must be addressed. Among the most important are:

    a. the amount of lease payment and how it is paid;

    b. which equipment is included in the lease;

    c. who is responsible for repair and maintenance of the equipment and facilities;

    d. who pays the common area maintenance costs;

    e. the duration of the lease; and

    f. which party is responsible for carrying fire insurance.

Chapter 6

1. Every foodservice owner/operator must make the decision as to what type of business organization is best for his or her enterprise.

2. All businesses are legally seen as proprietorships, partnerships or corporations, each with its own unique tax consequences that affect

    a. federal income taxes;

    b. liability to creditors;

    c. legal and/or personal relationships among owners; and

    d. legal life and transfer of ownership in the future.

3. A sole proprietorship is the simplest way to form a business organization. Owners are not treated as employees for tax purposes. Their income is based solely on profits from the enterprise. However, they must pay self-employment taxes.

4. A partnership accommodates several owners.

    a. In a general partnership, all members share in the management and liabilities of the company.

    b. In a limited partnership (often called a silent partnership), one or more parties have limited liability and no management decision making powers.

    c. Partnership income taxes are similar to those of sole proprietorships.

5. Corporations allow individuals to separate their personal assets from the business.

6. Additional funds can be raised by selling stock in the corporation, but to remain in control the owner must retain fifty-one percent of the company's stock.

7. Because it is considered a separate legal entity, a corporation is taxed on its earned income. Owners paid either a salary or dividends from the company are then taxed again.

8. To avoid double taxation, some owners choose to file as an S corporation. This is also a smart way to offset operating losses in the first few years of business.

9. A joint venture is set up especially for one business venture. This method offers each partner more flexibility. While the business operates for tax purposes as a partnership, each party can choose to file as an S corporation and divide income from the business to members of their respective family.

10. After choosing what type of business organization is right, owners must still meet and/or obtain a long list of requirements, permits, and licenses before opening their doors to customers. Among the most important are:
    a. zoning ordinances governing how and where a business can locate;
    b. local and state health code regulations which establish the standards every operation must meet;
    c. business licenses and tax registration;
    d. workers' compensation insurance; and
    e. federal workplace laws governing safety precautions and benefits given to employees.

11. To maximize cash flow, many restaurants use an accelerated depreciation method because it reduces taxes during the first few years of the business' life.

12. Restaurant owners can deduct a number of expenses from their taxes, including:
    a. attending industry-related meetings and conventions;
    b. a company-owned car;
    c. life and health insurance for executives and their families; and
    d. a van or bus used to transport employees to or from work.

13. All businesses with more than one employee must file with the IRS, obtain an employer identification number, and withhold federal payroll taxes.

14. It is very important for business owners to familiarize themselves with all federal regulations governing employment. These laws mandate not only the number of hours a week an employee can work, but also mandate that discrimination based on race, sex, or age is illegal.

Chapter 7

1. The menu is the controlling document in all foodservice operations. Designing the menu is the number one priority when opening a new restaurant. Because the restaurant concept is based on what guests in the target market expect, the menu must satisfy or exceed their expectations.

2. When planning a new menu, managers must remain aware of how each choice will affect different aspects of the restaurant. Choices must be matched with the
   a. capabilities of the chef;
   b. equipment to be used;
   c. availability of ingredients;
   d. customer's price-value perceptions;
   e. nutritional needs of patrons;
   f. contribution margins of each menu item; and
   g. flavors the target market will find intriguing.

3. A table d'hote menu allows patrons to build a complete meal at a fixed price.

4. Appetizers, soups, salads, entrees, and desserts normally are given their own section in the menu. Coffee shops often devote a separate section for breakfast foods, even if they are served all day long.

5. After all selections have been made, a menu analysis should be conducted to show a balance between items with a high food cost percentage and those with a low food cost percentage.

6. The layout, format, and paper a menu is printed on must match the operation's décor and theme.

7. Chefs and kitchen staff follow standardized recipes to ensure menu items are consistently prepared.

8. An operation's cost of goods consumed is found using the formula:
   Opening inventory + Purchases − Closing inventory = Cost of goods consumed

9. Food cost percentage is the guideline most owners use to determine their profitability. The food cost percentage is determined by using the formula:
Cost of goods sold − Total sales = Food cost percentage

Chapter 8

1. Each state has its own department of alcoholic beverage control (ABC), which regulates the manufacture, importing, and sale of all alcoholic beverages in that state.
2. There are basically two types of liquor licenses: a general license for all alcohol sales and another for serving beer and wine only.
3. To receive a new license, both the ABC and local governments must approve it.
4. Once the license is obtained, all liquor must be purchased from either a wholesaler or manufacturer.
5. The bar setup is divided into three areas:
   a. the front bar, where guests may sit and where the bartender mixes drinks;
   b. the back bar, which may be designed for aesthetics and to hold additional liquor; and
   c. the under bar, where main equipment such as the speed rack is located.
6. The design for a new bar will depend on the restaurant's concept: whether the bar will be a major retail area or a holding zone for guests waiting to be seated.
7. Selecting the right bartender is critical to the success of a bar because it is the bartender's responsibility to manage the operation and ensure that all liquor laws are followed.
8. The two most important qualities to consider when choosing the appropriate wine are richness and lightness.
9. Flavor and texture describe both food and wine, so light wines should be matched with light food.
10. Both the nose and the tongue determine flavor.
11. Developing and maintaining a responsible alcoholic beverage service program is of vital importance. If a problem with a patron does occur, be sure to document the situation.
12. Dram shop laws state that owners of establishments are responsible for injuries caused by intoxicated customers.

13. The penalty for serving alcohol to minors or intoxicated customers is severe and can be imposed on both the server and the owner of the restaurant or bar.

14. To avoid loss of alcohol through mishandling or theft, a weekly or bi-weekly audit should be conducted.

15. Restaurant owners must remain aware of the vast number of ways theft can occur in their establishments. Putting control systems in place will discourage most employees from theft and will make catching employees who do steal much easier.

Chapter 9

1. Once in place, an effective food purchasing system will help the entire restaurant run smoothly. To work properly, it must establish:

    a. product specifications;

    b. a method to control effort and losses;

    c. par stocks and reorder points for all items;

    d. the person in charge of the ordering process; and

    e. the person responsible for accepting and storing all deliveries.

2. Product specifications tell vendors exactly what characteristics are required for each food item ordered by the restaurant.

3. To determine when to order inventory items and how much to order, managers must forecast business volume. They then set a par stock (the minimum amount that should be on hand at any given time) and a reorder point (a time to place a new order based on the amount in stock) for every item in the inventory.

4. Orders are generally placed in the form of a purchase order listing the items to be delivered.

5. Some items might be delivered automatically at regular intervals with a standing order, used for perishable items such as milk.

6. To ensure product quality and cost control, each item must be stored in a proper location, maintained at the proper temperature, and issued before the end of its shelf life.

7. Most operations use the first-in, first-out (FIFO) issuing method in which older items are used before newly delivered items.

8. Meat items are chosen for their grade, determined by the United States Department of Agriculture (USDA), based on fat content, tenderness, and cost.

9. The quality of meat needed for each restaurant depends on the restaurant's concept.

10. Meat can be purchased as a whole carcass, wholesale cut, or in ready-to-serve portions.

11. Turkey usually yields more meat per bird than chicken, but if the menu explicitly states the dish is made of chicken, then chicken must be used.

12. Purchasing frozen eggs for baked goods is usually the best buy.

13. When choosing which grade of fresh eggs to purchase, it is best to determine the cost per ounce of each type of egg available.

14. To receive the quality of fresh fruits and vegetables that are right for the restaurant, the buyer must specify the grade, size, count, container size, and degree of ripeness. The USDA has set federal standards that help when making buying decisions.

15. Canned or frozen fruits and vegetables can often be substituted when baking or making soups.

16. Coffee flavors vary greatly between rich and robust to light, depending on where the beans were grown and how long they were roasted. The choice is based on the client's expectations. Some coffee manufacturers will install a brewing machine if the owner promises to order all the coffee from the manufacturer.

Chapter 10

1. A well-designed kitchen will
   a. minimize the number of steps taken by wait staff and kitchen personnel;
   b. accommodate the needs of workers and customers who are disabled, as mandated by federal regulations; and
   c. meet the sanitary guidelines established by the National Sanitation Foundation.

2. The most effective kitchen plan is rectangular in shape.

3. Open kitchens allow customers to observe the chef in action, but are more expensive to build because they require both an interesting piece of equipment to focus on and acoustical tile to reduce noise from the kitchen.

4. Kitchen floors should be made with materials that are nonabsorbent, easy to clean, and resistant to harsh chemicals.

5. Equipment is a major expense and investment for any foodservice owner, so its selection and maintenance is crucial. Equipment is selected to meet the operation's production needs, capacity of its staff, and financial resources.

6. All foodservice managers should be familiar with common pieces of equipment found in various areas of the operation.

   a. Reach-in refrigerator and freezer (storage area)

   b. Walk-in refrigerator and freezer (storage area)

   c. Mixer (pre-preparation area)

   d. Slicer (pre-preparation area)

   e. Peeler (pre-preparation area)

   f. Range (cooking area)

   g. Deep-fryer (cooking area)

   h. Tilting skillet (cooking area)

   i. Grill (cooking area)

   j. Ovens (cooking area)

   k. Steamer (cooking area)

   l. Broiler (cooking area)

   m. Food warmer (service and holding area)

   n. Steam table (service and holding area)

   o. Toaster (service and holding area)

   p. Dishwasher (clean-up area)

   q. Garbage disposer (clean-up area)

7. Several types of ovens are used in foodservice: low-temperature, forced convection, microwave, and infrared.

8. Not all equipment need be bought new. Restaurants close all the time, and used equipment with a long life ahead of it can be found, reducing costs.

9. All equipment must be cleaned and maintained regularly to ensure its longest life. This is especially true of the dishwasher, which requires constant maintenance. If it breaks down, not only will there be a short supply of dishware, but repairs often require waiting for a specialist to arrive. Some restaurants lease the dishwasher, leaving maintenance problems to the owner.

10. Whether a restaurant is newly constructed or replacing an existing restaurant, before the public can enter, it must pass inspections by public health officials and local planning boards.

Chapter 11

1. To determine if a restaurant will be viable, managers must develop a budget based on projected sales and operational costs. Creating this budget requires forecasting:
   a. Sales
   b. Cost of sales
   c. Gross profit
   d. Budgeted costs
   e. Labor costs
   f. Operating costs
   g. Fixed costs

2. Sales volume is determined by two factors:
   a. Average guest check—what each patron spends
   b. Guest count—number of customers over a specific period of time

3. Costs are divided into two categories:
   a. Fixed costs remain the same regardless of business volume and sales. These include real estate taxes, depreciation on equipment, and insurance.
   b. Variable costs change proportionately according to sales. Food and beverage costs go up or down depending on sales volume. The rent may also increase if sales exceed a predetermined amount stated in the lease.

4. Controllable expenses are those management can manipulate. They include payroll, direct operating expenses, and marketing.

5. Managers can control theft by establishing and enforcing "no ticket–no food" policies. They must also keep tight control on access to storage areas.

6. Computer systems have made many control activities much faster and are often more accurate for managers. However, information a computer provides is only as accurate as information put into the computer, and only as useful as the manager chooses to make it.

7. Computerized point-of-sale systems can improve efficiency and provide controls for handling cash.

8. Foodservice managers and lending institutions use ratio analysis to get a picture of an operation's financial success. To understand how the restaurant is doing at any given time, lenders look at the current ratio, which shows the relationship of current assets to current liabilities. The formula is:

Current assets − Current liabilities = Current ratio

9. Lenders also track the restaurant's quick ratio to be sure the company has access to sufficient cash to maintain operations.

Chapter 12

1. Before a foodservice operator can staff his or her operation, it is important to conduct a job analysis to determine which tasks will need to be performed. The two main approaches to job analysis are:

   a. bottom up, when the jobs already exist but still need to be defined, and

   b. top down, when opening a new restaurant.

2. The tasks and responsibilities developed through job analysis are written up as a job description for each position.

3. A job specification lists specific qualifications a person must have to perform tasks listed in the job description.

4. Tasks in each job description can be broken down into exact steps taken to complete the job. This information helps develop a system for training new employees, as well as a guide to evaluate the performance of each individual holding that position.

5. After each position is defined, an organization chart is created to show relationships among various jobs.

6. Several federal laws, including the Civil Rights Act, the Immigration Reform and Control Act (IRCA), and the Americans with Disabilities Act (ADA), regulate what employers may ask and require of employees.

7. Civil rights laws state that employers may not discriminate in employment on the basis of an individual's race, religion, color, sex, national origin, marital status, age, family relationship, mental or physical handicaps, or juvenile record (if it has been cleared.)

8. Equal employment opportunity is the legal right of all individuals to be considered for employment and promotion on the basis of their ability and merit.

9. The Equal Employment Opportunity Commission (EEOC) enforces laws requiring equal employment opportunity.

10. The Americans with Disabilities Act (ADA) provides civil rights protection for people with disabilities. The ADA defines a person with a disability to be an individual who falls within three categories:

   a. someone with a physical or mental impairment that substantially limits one or more major life activities;

   b. someone with a history of such an impairment; and/or

   c. someone who is perceived as having a disability.

   The ADA affects most employers, and all areas in a restaurant used by the public. By carefully matching jobs with the applicants' abilities, many restaurant owners now employ people who are physically or mentally challenged.

11. AIDS can not be transmitted through daily routines in a restaurant and is not a valid reason to refuse someone employment.

12. Recruitment, selection, and interviewing are the processes by which prospective employees are screened.

13. The interview process can be daunting for both the applicant and the employer. When making a hiring decision, remember that attitude is more important than ability.

14. Employment of minors is quite common in the foodservice industry. Some federal regulations control the kind of work minors (age 16 and younger) can perform.

15. The Immigration and Control Act of 1986 makes it illegal for employers to employ undocumented aliens.

16. Civil rights laws forbid discriminatory use of information in selecting employees. Text pages 323–324 list questions that should not appear on an application form or during an interview, as well as good questions that should be asked.

17. Careful selection of employees includes:

   a. checking references;

   b. employment testing, where it is valid and reliable; and

   c. screening out substance abusers.

Chapter 13

1. As it becomes more and more difficult to compete with other businesses for qualified and competent employees, foodservice managers must invest more resources—both time and money—in hiring, training, developing, and retaining the best people.

2. Training is no longer thought of as simply telling a new employee to follow a more experienced employee around for a day or two before getting started. The most successful operations have well-planned, thorough, and ongoing training programs for all employees.

3. A good training program begins with a systematic new employee orientation program meant to introduce new employees to the culture, environment, and shared values of the company. The orientation period is a chance for the operation to give a positive impression to new employees so they will give their new jobs their best efforts.

4. The overall goal of training is to instill proper attitude and develop job skills customers expect from the restaurant's employees.

5. Employee development gives employees the ability to come up with flexible solutions to problem situations.

6. For training to be effective, the trainer must be well acquainted with, although not necessarily proficient in, the tasks being taught.

7. The more tasks and jobs are broken down into separate steps, the more likely employees are to learn them.

8. Trainees must be given a chance to practice everything they are taught before having to perform these new concepts and skills on the job.

9. Learner Controlled Instruction (LCI) is a training system in which employees are responsible for learning new tasks and information at their own pace, and for completing tasks as a result. This can save management time and training costs.

10. Liquor liability is an area in which employee training is especially important. Dram shop laws make managers and employees responsible for accidents caused by customers who drive away from the operation while intoxicated.

11. Managers must also be effective leaders, encouraging and motivating employees to move the organization forward.

12. Leaders see problems as challenges and provide opportunities for their employees to overcome obstacles. However, if the same problems persist, employees will become frustrated.

Chapter 14

1. The most often cited reason customers give for not returning to a foodservice operation has nothing to do with food or prices or the competition—it is poor or indifferent service.

2. Servers have enormous power in the impressions guests have of an operation. Service has become the most distinguishing factor in this competitive industry.

3. Teamwork is an important part of good customer service. Managers must foster a work environment in which all employees recognize the important part they play in service.

4. Because servers earn more money from tips than paychecks, it is easy for them to see themselves as independent business people. This not only destroys teamwork but also can devolve into a game of one-upsmanship and destroy a customer's enjoyment of the restaurant.

5. The customer's first impression comes from the host or hostess at the front desk, whose main job is to welcome guests and facilitate seating arrangements.

6. The best server is a performer and a salesperson who attends to each detail and can manipulate events in such a way that the guest is left with a positive experience.

7. The formality or informality of employees must be appropriate for the particular operation's customers, theme, décor, and mission.

8. Servers can greatly influence the operation's profits—and their own tips—by "selling" the menu and its items. It is every manager's responsibility to train servers to give the best possible service, so customers will not only come back again and again, but tell their friends about the operation.

9. When employees hear complaints from customers, they should listen carefully to everything the customer says and act promptly to correct the situation.

10. Belligerent customers can be asked to leave, or the police can be called.

Chapter 15

1. A foodborne illness is a disease carried or transmitted to human beings by food.

2. One of the highest-profile areas of food service and public protection is food safety. When people get sick because of improperly prepared food, it usually makes the news.

3. The three types of food hazards are biological, chemical, and physical.

4. Biological hazards come from bacteria, which cause illness through pathogens. Pathogens are not harmful themselves but discharge toxins harmful to human beings and can infect people in three ways:

    a. intoxication from botulism, which can't be seen, smelled or tasted;

    b. infection such as salmonella, which can be transferred to humans from fowl or rodent droppings; or

    c. toxin-mediated infection, caused by organisms that lodge in the intestinal tract and discharge toxins.

5. Most foodborne illnesses are caused by high-protein foods improperly handled during the food preparation process.

6. The three most common foodborne disease-causing microorganisms are staph bacteria, salmonella and perfringens.

    a. Staph bacteria are spread by human contact and cannot be destroyed by high temperatures.

    b. Salmonella is most often found in eggs, milk and raw dairy products and can cause death.

    c. Perfringens, or the "cafeteria germ," grows well at room temperature. Even if a product is reheated, only the microorganisms are killed, leaving spores to come to life as the product cools.

7. Most foodborne illnesses can by avoided by simply keeping hands clean and following precautionary practices.

8. The best way to control or destroy bacteria is to heat food to at least 140°F and cool it quickly through the temperature danger zone of 41°F to 140°F.

9. Most bacteria are destroyed by heat. However, because microwaves cook foods unevenly, they are not safe places to reheat foods at risk of causing foodborne illnesses.

10. Viruses use food or human contact as a means of transportation and are rarely affected by heat. Outbreaks from viruses are often caused by poor personal hygiene.

11. Four types of chemical contamination can occur in a foodservice operation:

    a. detergents and sanitizers left on dishware;

    b. overuse of preservatives and food additives;

    c. toxic reactions from acidic foods held in metal-lined containers; and

    d. food contaminated by toxic metals.

12. Every restaurant should run a Hazard Analysis of Critical Control Points (HACCP) review to determine where contamination can occur and areas that need improvement.

13. The three most common food safety problems occur from food temperature abuse, cross-contamination, or poor personal hygiene. Managers must train all employees in safe foodhandling practices, including:

    a. proper delivery, storage, and cooking temperatures for food;

    b. strict adherence to personal hygiene standards; and

    c. cleaning utensils often, especially after working with high-risk foods such as raw chicken.

14. The federal Food and Drug Administration (FDA) sets guidelines for safe foodhandling procedures. All states use these guidelines to monitor restaurants for cleanliness and adherence to food protection ordinances. Those found in default can be shut down, and a notice may be placed in the local newspaper.

15. Warewashing equipment usually uses a combination of high heat and chemical sanitizers to keep dishes clean.

16. Most restaurant owners work with a professional pest control service to eliminate unwanted bugs and rodents.

Practice Test

This practice test contains 80 multiple-choice questions that are similar in content and format to those found on The Educational Foundation's final examination for this course. Mark the best answer to each question by circling the appropriate letter. Answers to the practice test are on page 85 of this student workbook.

Lesson 1: Introduction to Restaurant Operations

1. Restaurant owners believe that ultimately their success depends on
   A. the location of the restaurant.
   B. extensive advertising and promotions.
   C. hard work and excellent people skills.
   D. the design of the kitchen and dining room.

2. Family-owned restaurants have a better chance of surviving the start-up period because
   A. the cost of employing family members is lower.
   B. banks prefer to lend to family businesses.
   C. their children can eat for free.
   D. all their friends will prefer to dine there.

3. Lenders usually believe a loan to a new restaurant is
   A. no different than a loan to any other business.
   B. very risky, and often charge higher interest rates.
   C. an excellent investment and jump at the chance.
   D. acceptable, as long as the owners are a married couple.

4. The least expensive way to open your own restaurant is to
   A. build a new building.
   B. purchase a franchise.
   C. buy an existing restaurant and update its image.
   D. accept a management position with a large chain restaurant.

5. A number of franchises are increasing profits by
   A. rigorously maintaining their concept in overseas operations.
   B. saturating local markets.
   C. opening outlets in colleges and convenience stores.
   D. refusing to buy back franchises that fail.

6. The best way for a person to know if the restaurant industry is the right career choice is to
   A. open a fine-dining establishment.
   B. attend the National Restaurant Association trade show.
   C. read as many restaurant trade magazines as possible.
   D. work in a restaurant similar to the type he or she wants to own.

7. The goal of a quick-service operation is to
   A. serve the maximum number of customers in the least amount of time.
   B. help customers relax and enjoy the dining experience.
   C. develop menu items that truly reflect the restaurant's ethnic roots.
   D. encourage employees to invest in their skills and become franchise owners.

8. Theme restaurants fail due to
   A. a lack of public interest in the first few years of operation.
   B. food quality that is too high and cannot be maintained.
   C. celebrity owners selling off their investments.
   D. their inability to attract customers after the novelty wears off.

Lesson 2: Planning a Successful Operation

9. A new restaurant will have a better chance of beating the competition if it
   A. strives to be different and better.
   B. offers the same meals at a lower price.
   C. has a larger sign.
   D. stays open longer hours.

10. A restaurant's concept can be strengthened if the name chosen
    A. is a pun.
    B. sounds similar to the name of an established restaurant.
    C. establishes its identity.
    D. reminds people of a recent hit movie.

11. To discover whether or not there is a market for a new restaurant concept, it is best to
    A. hire a marketing firm to conduct a telephone survey.
    B. assess the number of people in the target market and determine their demographic profile.
    C. ask patrons at other restaurants in the area if they might be interested in your idea.
    D. discuss your idea with friends who live in the area and see what they think.

12. Which type of restaurant generally offers the most space per guest?

    A. Family restaurant
    B. Coffee shop
    C. Quick service restaurant
    D. Luxury restaurant

13. What type of foodservice operation tends to rely on public relations to promote the business?

    A. Family restaurant
    B. Coffee shop
    C. Quick service restaurant
    D. Luxury restaurant

14. Which of the following types of restaurants is most dependent on location for its success?

    A. Family restaurant
    B. Coffee shop
    C. Quick service restaurant
    D. Luxury restaurant

15. Which of the following information should not be included in a mission statement?

    A. The purpose of the enterprise
    B. The strategy of the business
    C. The expected behavioral and ethical standards
    D. The anticipated profit margin

16. Which of the following is considered a traffic generator?

    A. Wholesale warehouse
    B. Sports arena
    C. Bank
    D. Hospital

17. When examining a proposed site, how many knockout criteria are acceptable?

    A. Zero
    B. One
    C. Three
    D. Five

18. The selection of lighting design and color schemes for a restaurant is critical because

    A. they can be very expensive.
    B. people need to be able to read the menu.
    C. they interact to create the desired atmosphere.
    D. the wrong combination will show dirt too easily.

19. The tool a foodservice operation uses to communicate benefits it offers customers is called a

    A. mission statement.
    B. marketing plan.
    C. market analysis.
    D. demographic survey.

20. A well-defined marketing and business plan not only helps a restaurant succeed, but can also be used to
    A. obtain financing.
    B. eliminate competition.
    C. develop employee training manuals.
    D. streamline purchasing.

21. Which of the following is not one of the four Ps of a marketing strategy?
    A. Price
    B. Product
    C. Procurement
    D. Promotion

22. A foodservice operation aims its products, services, and marketing effort toward its
    A. regular customers.
    B. target market.
    C. entire community.
    D. city's tourists and conventioneers.

23. A serving of vegetarian lasagna costs $3.87 to make. Using cost-based pricing, what price should be charged to obtain a food cost percentage of 33?
    A. $11.60
    B. $12.50
    C. $13.85
    D. $13.99

24. Sales promotion is best described as
    A. materials meant to remind customers in the operation of what is available.
    B. efforts to communicate with the media and community.
    C. paid communications to the public.
    D. activities meant to persuade customers to visit the restaurant.

Lesson 3: Financing, Legal and Tax Matters, and Menu Considerations

25. The Small Business Administration
    A. lends money for new home mortgages to small business owners.
    B. guarantees loans to small businesses.
    C. finds banks willing to lend to small businesses.
    D. teaches owners of small businesses how to apply for a loan.

26. On a lease, CAMs refer to
    A. common area maintenance costs.
    B. clauses to amend marketing services.
    C. collateral assigned to a manager's discretion.
    D. contingent on approval by the municipal government.

27. When selling a restaurant, two values must be determined. The first is its real estate value and the second is its value as a

A. tourist destination.
B. job creator for the local community.
C. profit generator.
D. traffic generator.

28. Which type of business organization is the least complicated?

A. Partnership
B. Sole proprietorship
C. Joint venture
D. S corporation

29. The type of partner that has little liability and no management rights is called a

A. general partner.
B. management partner.
C. limited partner.
D. joint venture partner.

30. The primary advantage of an S corporation is that it

A. prevents the business from paying corporate taxes.
B. is the simplest form of business organization.
C. lets owners give gifts of stock to family members tax-free.
D. allows shareholders to deduct unlimited benefits from their taxes.

31. A relationship in which investors in one business team up with investors of another business to form a third entity is called a

A. general partnership.
B. limited partnership.
C. joint venture.
D. corporation.

32. Tax experts sometimes recommend that all real estate and equipment be put in an asset corporation to

A. avoid legal liability.
B. avoid paying corporate taxes.
C. dissolve the corporation more quickly.
D. maximize depreciation deductions.

33. Restaurant owners often use an accelerated depreciation method to

A. reduce taxes during the early years of the business.
B. buy new equipment sooner.
C. sell the business at a higher price.
D. avoid double taxation.

34. Which federal agency oversees anti-discrimination laws?

A. National Labor Relations Board
B. Food and Drug Administration
C. Equal Employment Opportunity Commission
D. Federal Trade Commission

35. To make sure a menu item is prepared with the same quality and quantity every time, restaurant owners rely on
    A. signature items.
    B. menu analysis.
    C. standardized recipes.
    D. product specifications.

36. Which of the following is commonly referred to as the "silent salesperson of the restaurant?"
    A. Menu
    B. Purchasing agent
    C. Manager
    D. Décor

37. School cafeterias typically use what type of menu?
    A. California
    B. Seasonal
    C. Cyclical
    D. Degustation

38. A restaurant had $19,884 worth of food in its inventory on June 1 and $18,762 on June 30. Its June food purchases totaled $25,604. What was the cost of food consumed for June?
    A. $13,042
    B. $26,726
    C. $48,003
    D. $64,250

39. The restaurant in the previous question had sales in June totaling $69,480. What was the restaurant's food cost percentage for June?
    A. 14.4 percent
    B. 29.1 percent
    C. 38.5 percent
    D. 41.9 percent

40. An operation's steak sandwich has a selling price of $10.95. It costs $3.41 to prepare. What is the item's contribution margin?
    A. $6.12
    B. $7.54
    C. $8.08
    D. $10.95

41. A single slice of pie costs one restaurant $0.65 to prepare. In order for the item to have a contribution margin of $2.35, the selling price must be
    A. $2.35.
    B. $2.50.
    C. $2.75.
    D. $3.00.

Lesson 4: Bar and Beverages and Food Purchasing

42. Before a restaurant owner can sell beer or wine, he or she must be granted a license from the
    A. Food and Drug Administration.
    B. Department of Alcoholic Beverage Control.
    C. Department of Agriculture.
    D. Drug Enforcement Agency.

43. The dram shop laws state that
    A. persons under the age of 18 cannot purchase alcohol.
    B. minors are not allowed to serve alcohol.
    C. applicants for a liquor license must notify the newspapers.
    D. owners are liable for injuries caused by intoxicated customers.

44. To avoid thefts of alcohol, most restaurant managers
    A. are also bartenders.
    B. conduct weekly audits.
    C. buy alcohol only from wholesalers.
    D. invest in a speed gun.

45. Restaurants use what tool to control the quality of the foods they purchase?
    A. Walk-in refrigerators
    B. Production sheets
    C. Menu analysis
    D. Product specifications

46. The amount of time a food product can be stored without a noticeable loss in quality is called its
    A. product specification.
    B. shelf life.
    C. par stock.
    D. reorder point.

47. A restaurant usually pays more for food items than a typical shopper because
    A. the supplier delivers and sells on credit.
    B. shoppers can use coupons.
    C. restaurants always receive higher quality fresh produce.
    D. restaurants offer foods that are out of season.

48. In order to make sure no stored food gets too old, restaurants use a
    A. first-in, first-out rotation system.
    B. last-in, first-out rotation system.
    C. first-in, last-out rotation system.
    D. last-in, last-out rotation system.

49. The agency that judges the quality of meats and establishes the grading system is the
    A. Food and Drug Administration.
    B. National Livestock and Meat Board.
    C. Department of Agriculture.
    D. Environmental Protection Agency.

Lesson 5: Planning and Equipping the Kitchen and Budgeting and Controlling Costs

50. According to the American Gas Association, the most efficient kitchen design is
    A. circular.
    B. square.
    C. rectangular.
    D. oval.

51. The conveyor broiler used by some hamburger quick service restaurants is an example of kitchen equipment that
    A. eliminates the need for cooking skills.
    B. is multi-functional.
    C. doubles as a centerpiece in an exhibition kitchen.
    D. cooks by circulating hot air.

52. The type of equipment an operation uses depends primarily on which of the following?
    A. The manager's cooking skills
    B. Average business volume
    C. Cash flow
    D. The menu

53. Which piece of equipment is most likely to be found in an operation's pre-preparation area?
    A. Broiler
    B. Steamer
    C. Slicer
    D. Range

54. Hamburgers are most often cooked on a
    A. range.
    B. griddle.
    C. tilting fry pan.
    D. steamer.

55. The top of a griddle is normally made from which metal?
    A. Cast iron
    B. Copper
    C. Steel
    D. Brass

56. Ideally, a griddle should preheat to 350°F or 400°F (177°C or 204°C) in
    A. 1 to 5 minutes.
    B. 7 to 12 minutes.
    C. 15 to 20 minutes.
    D. 40 to 45 minutes.

57. Which piece of equipment cooks food submerged in hot oil?
    A. Tilting skillet
    B. Steam-jacketed kettle
    C. Convection steamer
    D. Deep-fat fryer

58. In the foodservice industry, the "pot that thinks it's a griddle and a griddle that acts like a pot" is the

    A. tilting skillet.
    B. steam-jacketed kettle.
    C. microwave oven.
    D. deep-fat fryer.

59. Cooking meats for long periods at low temperatures has the advantage of

    A. reducing shrinkage.
    B. improving the flavor.
    C. bringing meats to the well-done stage more quickly.
    D. holding in the meat's juices.

60. Which type of oven cooks food with a fan that circulates hot air?

    A. Deck
    B. Convection
    C. Microwave
    D. Pizza

61. The Uniform System of Accounts for Restaurants is published by the

    A. Food and Drug Administration.
    B. Internal Revenue Service.
    C. National Restaurant Association.
    D. National Society of Certified Public Accountants.

62. A restaurant had total sales last year of $617,882 and costs totaling $537,040. What was the restaurant's gross profit?

    A. $78,004
    B. $80,842
    C. $82,376
    D. $84,552

63. To determine whether or not a restaurant is making a profit, the owner should examine the

    A. purchasing records.
    B. guest check averages.
    C. income statement.
    D. reservations book.

Lesson 6: The Human Side of Business and Food Protection and Sanitation

64. The list that describes the education level and technical skills a person needs to perform a job is called a

    A. task analysis.
    B. job description.
    C. job specification.
    D. job analysis.

65. Which of the following questions cannot be asked during an interview?

 A. Do you have a reliable means of transportation to get to work?
 B. Where were your parents born?
 C. What did you like the least about your last job?
 D. How long do you think you will be able to work here?

66. Which federal regulations make it illegal to discriminate against legal immigrants to the United States?

 A. The Americans with Disabilities Act
 B. The Equal Employment Opportunity Commission
 C. The Immigration Reform and Control Act
 D. The Department of Labor

67. Which of the following generally is true in an operation with a well-designed employee training program?

 A. Employees leave once their training is over.
 B. Employees who successfully complete the program are promoted to management.
 C. Employees are unclear about how their position fits into the organization as a whole.
 D. Employee turnover is lower.

68. Which of the following skills is most appropriate to train through behavior modeling?

 A. Operating a dishwashing machine
 B. Coordinating customer seating
 C. Interviewing job candidates
 D. Grilling steaks to order

69. In Learner Controlled Instruction, an employee's training is directed and monitored by the

 A. employee's supervisor.
 B. operation manager.
 C. employee.
 D. head chef.

70. The management trainee's "2½ times rule" refers to the number of times the

 A. trainee should visit a customers' table.
 B. trainee is permitted to take the management exam.
 C. trainer will demonstrate a task or job.
 D. trainer will evaluate the trainee's performance.

71. Which of the following behaviors is considered part of effective leadership?

A. Discussing an employee's mistakes in front of co-workers to set an example.
B. Sharing operational information with employees.
C. Accepting new ideas only from senior employees.
D. Talking with employees only when there are problems.

72. The number one reason why most customers say they will not return to a restaurant is because they

A. were unhappy with the quality of the food.
B. were unhappy with the quality of the service.
C. did not like the décor.
D. felt rushed during dinner.

73. When a customer complains about something to a server, the server should

A. ignore the complaint, unless a manager is nearby.
B. tell the customer it wasn't the server's fault, and tell the customer to whom their complaints should be directed.
C. assume that what the customer says is true and accurate.
D. explain what happened in the back of the house to cause the problem.

74. It is very important for managers to emphasize the need for servers to work as a team because

A. too often servers start to think of themselves as independent business people within the restaurant.
B. servers can start competing for tips and turn the customer/server relationship into a game.
C. teamwork improves the level of service in the entire restaurant.
D. all of the above.

75. To avoid foodborne illnesses, the temperature of cooked food should pass quickly through the

A. food danger zone.
B. bacterial end zone.
C. cooking zone.
D. thaw zone.

76. The Hazard Analysis of Critical Control Points helps foodservice establishments

A. reduce food costs.
B. identify employees' sloppy job performance.
C. eliminate pathogens from the kitchen.
D. reduce the incidence of sexual harassment.

77. Using the same knife and cutting board to chop vegetables and raw chicken is
   A. an efficient kitchen procedure.
   B. cross-contamination.
   C. a method to keep knives sharp.
   D. a highly developed skill.

78. Which of the following is a parasite often found in undercooked pork?
   A. Trichinosis
   B. Clostridium perfringens
   C. *E. coli*
   D. Streptococcus

79. Which micro-organism is called the "cafeteria germ" because it thrives in cooked foods held for service in food warmers?
   A. Salmonella
   B. Clostridium perfringens
   C. Trichinosis
   D. *E. coli*

80. The two facets of pest control are to kill pests once they are discovered, and to
   A. train employees in safe foodhandling practices.
   B. keep the temperature in the kitchen constant.
   C. keep to a minimum the number of employees in the kitchen.
   D. keep pests from entering the facility.

Practice Test Answers and Text Page References

1. C . . . . .p. 6	28. B . . . . .p. 152	55. C . . . . .p. 264
2. A . . . . .p. 8	29. C . . . . .p. 154	56. B . . . . .p. 264
3. B . . . . .p. 9	30. A . . . . .p. 157	57. D . . . . .p. 264
4. B . . . . .p. 9	31. C . . . . .p. 158	58. A . . . . .p. 265
5. C . . . . .p. 14	32. D . . . . .p. 159	59. A . . . . .p. 266
6. D . . . . .p. 15	33. A . . . . .p. 163	60. B . . . . .p. 266
7. A . . . . .p. 24	34. C . . . . .p. 171	61. C . . . . .p. 287
8. D . . . . .p. 42	35. C . . . . .p. 204	62. B . . . . .p. 283
9. A . . . . .p. 56	36. A . . . . .p. 181	63. C . . . . .p. 282
10. C . . . . .p. 57	37. C . . . . .p. 200	64. C . . . . .p. 311
11. B . . . . .p. 61	38. B . . . . .p. 207	65. B . . . . .p. 323
12. D . . . . .p. 76	39. C . . . . .p. 207	66. C . . . . .p. 316
13. D . . . . .p. 77	40. B . . . . .p. 192	67. D . . . . .p. 338
14. C . . . . .p. 81	41. D . . . . .p. 192	68. C . . . . .p. 347
15. D . . . . .p. 80	42. B . . . . .p. 213	69. A . . . . .p. 348
16. B . . . . .p. 84	43. D . . . . .p. 224	70. A . . . . .p. 348
17. A . . . . .p. 85	44. B . . . . .p. 224	71. B . . . . .p. 352
18. C . . . . .p. 95	45. D . . . . .p. 238	72. B . . . . .p. 360
19. B . . . . .p. 102	46. B . . . . .p. 239	73. C . . . . .p. 370
20. A . . . . .p. 103	47. A . . . . .p. 240	74. C . . . . .p. 362
21. C . . . . .p. 107	48. A . . . . .p. 242	75. A . . . . .p. 382
22. B . . . . .p. 107	49. C . . . . .p. 243	76. C . . . . .p. 386
23. A . . . . .p. 117	50. C . . . . .p. 253	77. B . . . . .p. 389
24. D . . . . .p. 118	51. A . . . . .p. 261	78. A . . . . .p. 381
25. B . . . . .p. 135	52. D . . . . .p. 259	79. B . . . . .p. 380
26. A . . . . .p. 143	53. C . . . . .p. 260	80. D . . . . .p. 397
27. C . . . . .p. 147	54. B . . . . .p. 264